OTHER
LATITUDES

POEMS

BRIAN BRODEUR

THE UNIVERSITY OF AKRON PRESS
AKRON, OHIO

11   10   09   08   07   5   4   3   2   1

LIBRARY OF CONGRESS CATALOGING-IN-PUBLICATION DATA
Brodeur, Brian, 1978–
  Other latitudes : poems / Brian Brodeur. — 1st ed.
    p. cm. — (Akron series in poetry)
  ISBN 978-1-931968-55-3 (pbk. : alk. paper)
  I. Title.
  PS3602.R6347O84 2008
  811'.6—DC22

                    2008021797

The paper used in this publication meets the minimum requirements of American National Standard for Information Sciences—Permanence of Paper for Printed Library Materials, ANSI z39.48–1984. ∞

ACKNOWLEDGMENTS
The author wishes to thank the editors of the following journals and anthology in whose pages many of these poems, often in different versions, first appeared:

Best New Poets 2005 (Samovar Press, 2005): "To a Young Woman in a Hospital Bed"; *Crab Orchard Review*: "Albino Horses," "Cherry Blossoms" (from "Snapshots 1"), "Lehinch" (from "Snapshots 2"); *Gettysburg Review*: "Blue Collar" (from "Snapshots 1"), "The Brunch," "Reunion" (from "Snapshots 2"), "The Last Swimmers"; *Meridian*: "Habitation of the Moon," "Late Harvest" (as "Nostalgia for the Make-Believe"); *New Orleans Review*: "Tall Trees, Still Water"; *Phoebe*: "Convicted Felon"; *Pleiades*: "Annunciation"; *River Styx*: "Pendolino"; *Smartish Pace*: "Narcissus"; *So to Speak: A Feminist Journal of Language and Art*: "Oleander and Deer"; *storySouth*: "After the Accident," "Holy Ghost" (both from "Snapshots 1").

"The Brunch" was the winner of the 2004 Joseph Lohman Award sponsored by the Academy of American Poets.

The following poems were included in *So the Night Cannot Go on without Us*, the 2006 White Eagle Coffee Store Press Poetry Chapbook Contest winner, published in 2007: "Albino Horses," "Annunciation," "Asters," "The Blind Hunter," "The Brunch," "Dürer's Rhinoceros," "Habitation of the Moon," "Homecoming," "Narcissus," "Oleander and Deer," "Pendolino," both "Snapshots," "Tall Trees, Still Water," and "To a Young Woman in a Hospital Bed."

The author is indebted to George Mason University's Department of English for granting him the 2004-05 Thesis Completion Fellowship and to the generous support of the Key Charitable Trust. Heartfelt thanks to Vermont Studio Center and to the Johnson Center Library at George Mason University for granting him valuable leave time to write. Grateful acknowledgment is made to Elton Glaser and Stephen Dunn for choosing this manuscript as the 2007 winner of the Akron Poetry Prize, and to Mary Biddinger and Amy Freels at the University of Akron Press. In addition, the author would like to thank the following individuals who have helped shape these poems and this manuscript, and whose friendship and support have sustained him: Jennifer Atkinson, Matt Burriesci, Kiley Cogis, Bill Coyle, Dave Fenza, Carolyn Forché, Carrie Grabo, Brian Heston, Sally Keith, Peter Klappert, Chris Mabelitini, Semezdin Mehmedinović, Eric Pankey, J.D. Scrimgeour, Chris Tanseer, Alycia Tessean, Susan Tichy, and Melissa Tuckey.

Cover: Philip Pearlstein, "Nude on Iron Bench," 1975, Edition 50, 22" x 28" paper size, 18" x 24" plate size, Copyright Philip Pearlstein.

Contents

For Mark and Regina Brodeur
and for Kiley, with love

Even in this world more things exist without
our knowledge than with it and the order
in creation which you see is that which
you have put there, like a string in a maze,
so that you shall not lose your way.

—Cormac McCarthy, *Blood Meridian*

Annunciation

The Friesians are calving again. It is that season
of awaiting the difficult births. His father calls out
for Thomas to fetch the jack and tooling iron:
tendrils of flesh dangle from her hinds as the first
hoof kicks through. If it is male, it will be sold for slaughter.
If female, stolen away—dragged if necessary
by the legs—and locked with the others
in the wailing pen. For now, at least, there is one hoof
entering or leaving: either one is right. His father
jamming his hand in the throttled womb
to heave this bucking, usable thing into existence
before it slaps headfirst onto the concrete.
There is always, like this, the miracle. Then there is after.

1

The Blind Hunter

News Herald, *Woodhaven, NY, December 14, 2003*

I've seen him Sundays stalking
the reservoir, out for the day (or night, it doesn't matter)
negotiating castellated ridges, blue mantles

of pine. Last week, the crack of his Winchester
scared a tree of mourning doves half-crazy,
and I went down to see if the old man was all right.

From the folds of brush, he stumbled
into the light, a whitetail fawn draped over his shoulder.
Deep down he must know the whole thing's foolish:

chasing some whim could drive him off a cliff.
But what else is there for him? He has no kids, buried
his wife last year. I think of them together

lumbering through high grasses: her polished rifle
glinting, his dog let loose, waving their hands at me
like a couple drowning. They had a system:

she'd tap his knee once when the deer came close, twice
when he was pointed in the right direction, sliding
her finger in circles across his thigh

to two or three o'clock, then tap three times
when the deer stepped into range, four times to shoot.
He must've memorized the sound

of boots crackling in the brush. (I'm sure he knows
the smaller, sharper crackling of the deer.) Some days
I follow his trail to see what he does out there, how he'll fare

in the endless mesh of ferns, the early ice,
trudging up the hillock through the leaves.
And as we breathe the same cold wind

blown off the reservoir, it's as if I'm waiting for him
to disappear into the sunken goldenrod.
Waiting for him to duck down in some blind

only he knows exists, to turn and wave
or pull the trigger when he feels—who knows?—
his wife's hand tap four times against his thigh.

Asters

Not that they flourish
in hoarfrost, or flare up, bract
to bud, from blacktop
cracks (I know
none will keep), but that each
petal glisters without
meaning to, spreads its spiny
roots through chaff, unfurls
in cold clusters, tussocks
shaking, feeds
on ditch water, the sweet
decay found there.

Pendolino

Florence to Innsbruck, 1998

We scoot to make room, four strangers
lumped together, and trade stories as we watch
evening break against the man-faced Alps:

Harun from Sarajevo asks in English
if we've seen Verona yet, describes the bronze
statue of Juliet whose left breast shines green-gold—

polished over time by tourists' hands.
Claus laments forgetting to pack linens, confesses
to crabs he contracted at Amsterdam's Flying Pig,

making Maria, the only girl, squirm in her seat.
Maria asks Harun about the war. He says he wasn't there,
but his uncle Miljenko, starving, was forced

to slaughter the dog, cut the toughest meat
into strips they grilled on sticks and called
bat wing so his cousins would eat.

During the siege on Hamburg, Claus says, his father's
family stewed tulip bulbs to survive, once traded
a rancid melon rind for a pair of shoes.

I tell the story dad told me about the private
outside Dac To, how he crossed into Cambodia
to stalk Viet Cong regulars, taking each man

by the throat, whispering into his ear the name
of a dead friend, and sticking the blade just
under the left shoulder until he felt

the heart through the knife's hilt stop beating. Soon
we're all playing this game: whose people
suffered more, passing a bottle of peach schnapps

as we pitch through mountain tunnels, exploding
into fog. In the brightening window, a few Alpine firs
smack the flanks of the train. Our reflections

blur against whitecaps that slowly erase our faces,
and we lean on our packs, trying to stay awake,
as if the night could not go on without us.

Oleander And Deer

Sprawled on lawn chairs, we watch
a whitetail buck slip through pines.
His antlers seem brittle as coral

as he nibbles leaves off a sapling oak
and laps mud puddles, ignoring
the huge white blooms of oleander.

My mother retired at sixty from D.S.S.—
taking other people's kids away, she'd call it.
In the TV-light of our kitchen,

we used to cringe at her work stories,
what passed for normal family conversation:
abusive dads, neglectful moms, another infant

rushed to the ER with a broken hip.
Now, the garden is her life: the birdbath
clogged with blossoms, the odor of fresh mulch.

Amazing, she says; lovely, I agree,
as the deer's tail flicks at flies, one backlit ear
resembling the gnawed petal of a rose.

She doesn't think of herself as a gardener,
though she spends most summer days
tearing wildflowers from the fields, loves

to watch kudzu choke the earth, loves that deer
devour part of her labor, that the beautiful
oleander is too poisonous to touch.

To a Young Woman
in a Hospital Bed

It starts with an urge, she says, innocent
enough: clipping her fingernails
to the cuticle, paper cuts

she slits along her hands, or scratching up
her arms in homeroom with a plastic knife
to scare the gawking boys.

Eraser burns: those competitions
to see which of her girlfriends
flinches first as she scrapes the rubber

edges across her forearms, biting
down on a wooden ruler
so she won't scream, or stop.

Then she gets good at it: she always wins.
She does it on her own, rubbing
the eraser over black scabs, trying

to wipe away her own skin.
She experiments with safety pins, pricks
the soft flesh between index finger

and thumb, fastens them, sticks
five at a time, all in a row, and watches them
throb in a kind of dance.

She shows her friends who laugh
but cringe after she forces the eighth
pin through. And this is how she knows

something is wrong, carving the names
of rock bands into her thighs
with her stepfather's box cutter:

Poison, Aerosmith—it doesn't matter,
it just feels better cutting words
instead of marks that don't mean anything.

And this suffices, this becomes
what life is, hurt by hurt: pressing a hot
clothes-iron against her arm, lifting it

to let the steam breathe out.
She presses it down again, longer this time,
harder, as the burning fills the hall.

Minutes go by. And she feels
nothing. It's as if she's burning
someone else's skin, hot metal

peeling away another's flesh, scorching it.
She watches the skin singe, the muscle
bubble, but she still can't feel a thing.

So she stops, wraps the arm in gauze,
and goes on with her day, even forgetting
what made her want to do that to herself.

And in a way this makes it all
worth it: the fever, the infection, the dizzy
drive to the ER she hardly remembers,

the morphine drip, and the intern psych major
who asks her questions from a standard form
(even flirts with her a little),

the swell of pride she feels when she turns over
to show the scars—the deepest ones, the ones
branded on her back not even she has seen.

Dürer's Rhinoceros

A friend tells me weak minds find only metaphors in nature. *Cold iron,* we say, *cold bones* when the cricket settles in plantain lilies. Precarious, stippled leaves: who knows what lives out there, what breeds in the undergrowth, how it survives. The staves of its huge ribs. Its flesh piled on its frame like garniture. Did anyone berate Dürer for never having *seen* the beast he'd drawn? Or the author of Revelations? Or those artists' renderings of wanted men? No moon tonight, no wind, no weather at all. Looking up, we follow the trail of sky through pine tops, walk as far as the old fire road, decide to turn back. Here, he says, there used to be a farmhouse and hay barn, stables where they kept palominos. Now there's trees.

Albino Horses

Dipping their pink mouths in peat sludge soft as butter,
they edged what seemed the margins of an age

we'd read up on in our one, coverless copy
of *Let's Go: Ireland*. This pair of feral mares, displaced

or fugitive, grazing among beached shopping trolleys
and sacks of turf. Sporting our Aran sweaters

and gaiters bought off the B&B, who besides us would've noticed
the dried mud cracking with each hoof-clap, this tangle of

cedar roots gripping granite boulders like ribs around a lung?
When a pheasant screeched, they shifted, thrashing their tails

as they clattered over stones, their bright thighs
shuddering, and everywhere, the odor of turned ground.

The Brunch

It is much the way you said it would be, the world without you.
After the decision not to make a fuss, after the mass

and limo ride home for a change of clothes,
we walk through the pristine doors of the new Ramada Inn:

pitchers of ice water and OJ swaddled in cloth napkins,
rhubarb salad bleeding on a silver tray.

You'd wanted to know—as we all want to know—the details
that survive you: whether or not your ex-wife would show,

which maverick relative would speak first through their spumoni,
who would weep. In the background, a few crackling speakers

play something you'd have been ashamed to call music.
Your brothers and I, moaning into our drinks, nod about the day

you lured the stray with a bowl of poisoned meat
and smashed its twitching head with your father's hammer.

Population control, one of them grunts.
Only your mother seems alone with her violent grief,

bowed over the fruit salad, unable to lift the spoon: that feeling
of vacancy you spoke so shyly of over beers that morning.

An emptiness, you said, *not like a hunger so much as a*
cancer after it's been removed. The honeydew. The mango.

The roast dribbling its unwarm juices onto the bleached-
white linen. The stain vaguely resembling a map.

Snapshots 1

1. HOLY GHOST

My mother spreads tinsel snow over the kitchen sills,
sets the cedar manger in its place, arranges

the hollow plastic magi next to a cradle
displaying the baby Jesus missing an arm.

The little enameled figure of Mary kneeling
embraces something only Mary sees. Pinned to the banister,

our crocheted stockings sag. All afternoon,
mom listens to laundry click in the pantry dryer, packs

layers of chocolate cake and homemade cream
into Tupperware for the Heath-Bar trifle we love.

Light moves across the counter, almost touching her hand,
shattering over an open drawer of knives.

2. *BLUE COLLAR*

He never swore at us.
When I romped
through the wet cement
he'd been laying himself all Saturday,
he took me simply by the arm,

stopping his fist midair,
and pinned my skinny body
against the wall
with words I'd never heard
but understood.

Never *upset* or *angry*,
he was either *irate*, *livid*,
stern, or *cross*,
as the tiny veins around his temples
throbbed in unison.

I knew his separate smells
of aftershave and sawdust
and could hear
a kind of tenderness like guilt
quiver in his throat.

3. *CHERRY BLOSSOMS*
    for J. 1975-2000

You hated this time of year: when horsetail
ferns have just uncurled and sway as if underwater,
when the woods are not quite empty, not quite full,
and cottonwoods spill their seed against the mulch.
Our sets of pushups on the basement floor,
performing in the mirror before school. How much
time did we spend alone in the dark down there,
sweating in the cold? Dead leaves of the burgundy
ficus lined the wall, collecting in jagged piles.
You said it yourself about the cherry blossoms—
Shame we don't have time to adjust to this—
as they loose themselves in a heavy wind
and dapple the patio: the tremble and click of the limbs,
that green haze before the leaves come in.

4. *AFTER THE ACCIDENT*

As she clutches the metal ribs of the hospital bed—
still dreamy with pain and the morphine drip

they've started to wean her off—my sister
sucks ice chips from the nurse's latex hand.

From her room on the fifth floor, she's watched rainwater
pool and dissipate on tar-streaked roofs, heaves

of cloud-shadow drag across the courtyard
where shirtless men clear last season's leaves.

The fresh-stitched wound above her collarbone
bristles like a caterpillar. Her dark hair

spreads its root system over the pillow, and her eyes
open and close, rolling back in her head.

Imago

Far north, a family sits down to dinner. Dad scoops a spoonful of applesauce for himself, peers out the window at his fields. Time for another inventory. Count heads at the table, count asters and old roses, hay bales waiting on the grass (each one crowned with frost). Count steps in the dark for which there is no guide. In the east, Orion arrives, bringing again the scent of snow, like a man who wakes one evening far from home, surprised to find himself in his boyhood bedroom: same white walls, same heavy oak door, same highway sounds muffled through pines. This is the time of night when stars and houselights shine. The glitter of passing cars and freightliners. Mostly stars.

The Body

The whole county heard. Schiappucci and me
found her first out back of the old Shell station
and used a hockey stick to fish her out:

a young Hispanic girl, face up, legs splayed,
her hair threaded with bits of yellow grass.
Stabbed, strangled, raped (and, I heard,

in that order), she must've drifted all night
to have ended up so far downstream, miles
from Rainbow Terrace, where she'd lived.

When her brothers came, all seven of them,
to I.D. the body, no one, not even the cops,
had tried to move her. Schiappucci said

she worked at the Howard Johnson's off Quinsig.
He'd seen her—a pretty thing—down Bronzo's Bar,
running beers and wings to Keno players.

Days later, dozens of those cheap glass candles
with the Virgin Mary painted on the sides
gathered into a makeshift funeral pyre

spewing wax all over the concrete landing
where they first laid the body out to dry:
tiny flickering points of yellow light

you could see burning for weeks. One night,
I headed out with Schiappucci for a drive
and decided to walk down and have a look.

We found a break in the woods beside the stream,
groped through the dark toward the candlelight
where two women sat in lawn chairs.

Praying with their eyes open, they hunched over
photographs of the girl at different ages,
and tossed flowers into the smoky water.

Schiappucci thought of going down to them.
I thought of the girl's face the color of wax paper.
How her eyes stared at the sky, as if it mattered.

I couldn't move, couldn't say a word
until Schiappucci asked what time it was
and what did we come here for again so late.

The Last Swimmers

He goes under—it's all he can think to do—
    waits for his feet to touch bottom, clutches
her ribs and lifts her like a dancer

      above the steaming surface so she can breathe.
Parting the muck, he takes no small pleasure
    in feeling her arms squeeze his neck, her breasts

pressing against his back as he starts
    to paddle. She slides her hand down his chest
to grip him tighter, and he's convinced

    he can open his throat and swallow the whole
lake down, guzzle the grainy blackness, gulp
    by gulp, until they could walk back to shore.

Her breathing matches his. Is she humoring him?
    Her hair spills over his shoulders and sticks to his lips.
Farther in, his toes kick the mud below. So what

    if he keeps swimming, carrying her, weighted
down by this strange lust he feels for the thrill
    of her fingernails, her body slapping his?

Isn't this what he'd wanted, a task he could not fail?
    Gliding together, they come close enough
to touch the moon, making it ripple where it floats.

2

Figure Drawing

1.
I dreamed last night I died and was reborn
as a grain of sand in a clam's mouth
and that no one could find me

buried in that tightest deepest dark.
In the dream, I knew I'd died
and had been reborn before.

Once as a shard of glass
scattered the moment someone smashed
a church window with a baseball bat.

Again as a baby sparrow in the driveway
whose parents, with little bits of worm,
kept feeding and feeding it.

I knew all the bodies, the different
lives, had simply fallen away,
that I was somehow safer in the dark

and never had to die, grow old or fat,
or finish high school even, which was fine.
Until I woke to the chirp

of my mother's mattress
and knew I was back in her cramped apartment
that smelled like an airport,

back in another one of my stupid lives:
my mother wearing her cheap Chinese robe,
the dog's claws clicking across the floor

after the poor bitch had waited all night
for someone to just get up and notice her,
put their hands on her a little, and let her out.

2.
He was never my boyfriend, not
really. His letters were crazy:
I liked that about him. I even saved

my favorite sections, and a few
of his sketches—as evidence.
Sometimes I'd leave them out

for anyone to see.
It wasn't like I wanted him
to write. It made me sad for him:

*You asked why I wept the other night while you undressed. I used to have
control over my feelings. (I used to pride myself on just how much control
I thought I had.) But when I watched the robe fall from your shoulders
and slide down the meat of your back, there was such a glare. . . . It was
like opening a door onto snowfall—that violent whiteness; the paleness of
your back—and I had no control over it, I had no control over any of it.*

*My work, your body—I see no difference now. People like you and I—peo-
ple of feeling—for us, art is a pleasure that must be suffered through.*

3.
I'd seen the ad in the college catalogue: Model
Wanted. And right away I thought
this was something I could do, something

no one would *picture* me doing.
I started posing there, volunteering
my body. Two times a week, I'd just show up

wearing one of my mother's robes,
walk across the cold linoleum
of his studio, untying the robe as slow as I could,

trying hard to make it look pretty.
All the students watching acted like
I was nothing, staring at me

without seeming like they wanted to. Soon
I got so good he started keeping me
after class. Then calling me at home.

4.
Botticelli first appeared to me in the winter of 1972. I was alone in my
father's library where I spent most afternoons. (I do not know why I feel I
need to tell you this; ignore it if you want—perhaps I would prefer that!)
He came in a flourish of color I could feel all over my body: blood-reds and
blues. He had no hands—none that I could see. And when he opened his
mouth to speak, instead of words shards of stained glass came spilling out,
tearing his mouth to lace.

5.
He wore a beard and fancy
silk shirts. I first thought he was gay.
When he talked, he held his mouth

crooked, like he wasn't saying
what he wanted to say.
He'd give me suggestions

on how to relax, how to let the students
discover my body, *claim it*
as their own.

Think of it, he'd say, *not in terms*
of the motionless—a body is never still—
but in terms of movement, dance.

Keep your body perpetually
engaged; think of it as your instrument: a body
is never static, so why draw it that way?

6.
You tease me, you know you tease me, and that is our dynamic. Laugh! I
only wish you'd laugh at me; I would laugh if I saw what you see: a fool
arguing with himself about himself. An Exit sign above a locked door.

What do you see in the prints mounted on the wall? The woman chased by
soldiers, a dog clamping down on her. The goddess who floats on her cock-
leshell, still young and beautiful after five centuries!

7.

When I am watched, studied, I feel
inspired. There were moments of entire
collaboration, when his eyes

understood the thickness
of my belly, the lines of my body,
and the spirit underneath, the energy,

came through with every new
gesture I made: wearing my mother's
expensive perfumes, trying

not to show too much at once.
When I sat for him alone, I started to see
my role in history: a *Rebirth of Venus*

posing on her shell, the angel
and the man with puffed-out cheeks
waiting for that moment I'd arrive

reborn, a masterpiece. I started
to really crave our nights together.
Every time he came, I knew it was real.

He excused himself
like he'd done something wrong,
but I knew what we were doing

couldn't be wrong. I wasn't even
connected to my body anymore, but a kind of
dispossession—our different energies

mingling, unidentifiable, becoming
two pieces, shards,
broken from one whole.

8.
*Portrait painting. You say it like a breakfast cereal, as if it had no poetry
for you.*

*I know your body as a lover would. I could not bear to give myself over to
bowls of fruit. Disembodied torsos. No flesh in them. I feel I am becoming
your body more and more, by way of my restraint. The more I tie my pas-
sions down, the more they build and writhe.*

9.
Every time he came, letting it
drip all over the paint-stained floor,
I'd feel my body

come back to me, a little
misfigured, foreign,
and I knew I'd become

perfected, another form
visible in the light. It wasn't even
sexual anymore. The act, the idea of it,

had nothing to do with me
anymore. Watching him watch me,
I could see the blood

beat harder in his wrists. Cigarette ash
caught in his knuckle hairs as he
reached to touch me.

Stay with me, he'd say
after he finished. But how could I
when he was paying me?

And if I let him, if he took me
home one night, how could it be
beautiful after that? How could it be real?

3

Homecoming

He watches the porch spider
ascend and descend each silk rung
to inspect her bundles of thread

half-eaten on the swaying web.
Nothing truly wasted, nothing
scorned, she lets her egg sacks

mellow in the sun, spending
her days waiting, her nights with
small repairs. Seeing her climb

and shake on this silver mesh,
what harm in reaching to touch
her work, letting the damp silk

stretch as he thrums the web-lace
lightly with one finger, trying
to imitate the struggling fly?

Snapshots 2

1. *REUNION*

After a week of rain, another blue fog
breaks over the bay. Then the illusion of spring:

a last snowflake leaves its print on the windshield,
slight as the foot of a bird. Clasping hands,

we watch as the land relaxes,
easing soccer fields from forest edge.

Between stubble grass and rotted leaves, amaryllis
carves a place for itself—half of each placental bulb

splitting open the earth. Once,
there was the fear you would not return.

Then the fear you would. The happiness
that comes only from work (wadded-up papers

behind the desk) and the memory of your breasts:
the color of the sea at night—no—of broken stone.

2. *LEHINCH*

We slept against the burnt-out
hollow of an alder, drunk
on the last of your father's *poitín*.

Above us, autumn's static
hushed what was left of the leaves.
Culled into a corner of

the aluminum barn, the blind heifer
dreamed of silage on her bed.
All night the cows

made sea sounds
in another world. Cattails, stiff
as matches, broke the breeze.

3. *LAST SUMMER IN GALWAY*

Nights, he'd lay waiting for her
to walk home from work and open the bedroom door,
carrying with her the odors of Supermacs.
He'd watch her tug at the thick elastics
as the bell-ropes of her braids slowly unraveled
and she collapsed on her side of the bed.
What was it they said to each other—what was left to say?

The drugged winds of August hauled in off the bay.
The Burren swallowed its turloughs of rainwater,
each night drinking deep from the limestone's center.
He'd lean in close to smell the grease still sour in her hair
as she nodded off and pressed her fists together
against her chest—not in prayer but as if she held
a last crust of bread, or a pulsing bird.

4. *THE BARN OWL*

dives to life, parting the boughs,
and plunges past our heads, talons
splayed, to wrench

vole or mouse from an icy hole.
I squeeze my fists, jerk
back, and whatever thought or feeling, whatever

light the moon gave off,
dissolves into the action of the owl.
As you clutch my arm, we talk the whole way home

of Audubon: how carefully he must've held
their bodies, needle between his teeth, as he
unfurled their dark insides into a dish,

filling their wings with flax and gauge wire
to pose upright and sketch each one
on the perch as if in motion.

Late Harvest

1.

I saw her again this afternoon
in someone else's body—
same faded denim coat, same

hair the color of dry grass—
standing beside the overpriced azaleas.
I remember us that Fourth of July

watching the half-drunk
firefighters bury the slaughtered
hog on a bed of coals,

cover it in earth, and wait
eight hours to dig up the charred
flesh we all devoured.

How beautiful she was
with a mouthful of pig:
clad in her paper bib,

her can of Bud stuck in a tie-dyed
beer-warmer that read
Breakfast of Champions.

2.

"I love you," some guy cries out, "you fucking bitch!"
"Fuck you," she screams. "You couldn't stop staring at Jennifer's tits."
"I love you," he says again. "Come sit next to me in the truck."

The last motorboat of teenagers empties onto the dock.
Their life preservers flash as they fumble from a broken stepladder,
hauling huge plastic coolers and fishing rods that stab the air.

I see her often now (I never used to): walking a chocolate lab
or gazing at her nails in a Honda Civic behind me at the light.
Sometimes she's better looking, sometimes not.

Convicted Felon

1.

If we argued that night, it was about nothing:
plans, her makeup, the usual shit.
Other girls I wasn't looking at.

Whose turn it was to drive
whatever we drove that night
into a ditch. Truth is,

if you asked me the color of her eyes
I couldn't say, or how we *were* together
when she was alive.

It was her idea
to play Bonnie and Clyde.
To jack that Nissan from the lot

and just drive. And in a way I guess
we were Bonnie and Clyde.
Saying it to each other, saying the names

gave us permission to crawl inside
their legend and their lives.
But I wouldn't change it, not even now.

She was the type I thought you only
saw on TV, who reads
L'Amour books on the toilet

and pisses in the woods. She said
she would've swallowed glass for me
if I asked her to. But why would I?

2.

I remember my father, his words:
Sex is in the Bible, he'd say, *a mechanism for
change, a key to a pair of handcuffs.*

The first car I jacked was with him,
who had nothing better to give.
He got the shakes so awful in his hands

and for the first time in my life,
he really needed me.
I knew he'd be gone again soon,

that I wouldn't hear the shotgun engine
of his snores booming from his room.
Or watch him shave in the middle

of the night without any lights.
But I didn't start living, really living,
until I jacked one on my own.

Broad daylight. I couldn't help it.
Seeing them all glow like candy
in perfect rows along the street,

I got the itch for it (it's like an itch).
I found one that was open—*open!*—
cracked the plastic steering

column, tore out the barrel ignition's
greasy hairs, twisted them together,
and made her purr straight across the state.

3.
But it was always how she wanted it,
how she thought it should be:
in the shed with our shirts on—

her wanting it to be better and better,
telling me girls don't like it
as much at first, and to go

easy. Holding her by the hips,
I slid inside her slow, watching her eyes
stare off in a kind of frenzy.

First time, I was seventeen and she was twenty.
She said there was a place behind
the Cineplex where we could see the city.

Even then I knew I wasn't the first
she used that on. We walked out
past the strip mall dumpsters,

away from the cars in a little gully
beside the highway. Once,
she brought a thing of coconut oil

I rubbed all over her skin
until she glowed like a seal,
and it was funny.

4.
After we wrecked, the rain
made the pavement hiss, made everything
under the streetlights shine:

the cracked windshield, the blinking
lights, oil piddling onto the asphalt.
And just like that, I knew

I was alive. Then I felt
bone poking through my shin, tasted
gasoline in the back of my throat.

I pulled her shirt up over her face
to cover her. She had nothing
on underneath. As the highway

flickered around us, I watched the city
turn on, listened to the filth
flowing below us in the river.

I remember thinking it was strange
that the light was what covered us in shadows.
The light from the parking lot

glittering across the unliving water—
that someone, just like that, could be
forgiven what he's done.

Straw Man

Some nights, a certain rhythm in the wind,
      he is moved almost to dancing.
Shaking on stakes, his coat rustles and his seams
      loosen, scattering

silage on the ground. He feels field mice burrow
      through his chest, the heat
of bodies nesting there, as stars, little perforations
      in the sky, flare into celestial peepholes.

He wants to close his drawn-on eyes.
      In the chitter of corn leaves, stubble
columbines and asters, he hears
      promises: how he, too, will ascend

into the Heaven of his kind where, at harvest time,
      they stuff their makers with straw,
tie them with wire, and watch the storms
      take without asking.

Near the Fountain of Tears

carve a moment
out of dream stone
for the poet in the Alhambra,
over a fountain where the grieving water
shall say forever:
The crime was in Granada, his Granada.
　　　　—Antonio Machado

The rooms, still dark, were flooded
　　　　with blue shadows
when Tripaldi bound
　　　　the two bullfighters together.

I chained the lame
　　　　schoolteacher and the man
with a swollen head—as Alonso called him—
　　　　who even thanked me

for letting him step on my knee
　　　　as he climbed onto the flatbed.
We drove along a ravine
　　　　to a stretch of hillside

studded with olive trees, unloaded
　　　　the prisoners there,
and led them down the mud
　　　　where the slope

leveled. Unsnapping my canteen,
　　　　I offered it to the man,
who drank and spilled on his shoes.
　　　　Tripaldi told him he'd seen

a play of his performed in Barcelona.
      "The one about all those
unhappy women," Tripaldi said.
        The man grinned and looked at me.

"Most women I know," he said,
      "are unhappy,
especially Spanish women."
        "My friend," Tripaldi laughed, "I agree."

The sun had not yet risen
      when the command was given.
The prisoners stood in silence, shoulder
      to shoulder, as we cocked our rifles.

The man with a swollen head
      fell suddenly, hitting the wet ground
a moment before the schoolteacher's
      body fell on his.

Then the two bullfighters—
      all of them lying
together in the muck—and we dragged
      their bodies by the shackles,

forming a straight line, waited for
      the diggers to climb
down with their spades. As the sun
      rose over the *vega*,

we smoked and watched the sky
            come back to life. When the diggers finished,
we heaved the bodies to the edge, a few
            beads of my sweat

dripping onto the man's face. Tripaldi
            asked if I'd ever killed anyone
famous before. "No," I said,
            and rolled them into the hole.

Lost River

Hearing floodwaters rise, would we
      dive into the bilge
    and float with the cold current,

feel our lungs flood, our voices
      gutter? Or climb some roof
    to spot those final

stars blinking out, as we wait for one big
      swell to roll us under?
    Either way, no one would live to see

those wakes unfreeze, no new race
      discover us encased in the floes
    as if in amber, or wonder

who we were, or marvel at how
      glad in our flesh we seemed.

Late Fugue, or Poem Ending with a Phrase by Marvin Bell

In a warehouse of sequestered instruments,
a teenage boy and girl hurry out of
their clothes. She tries yanking his trousers

over his shoes and he falls down laughing.
She laughs, too, and their voices fill
the room: each chuckle strikes the flanks

of an old clavier, awakening the vast
and complex innards of a drone
harmonium, flugelhorns, bells.

As they crawl under a dusty Bösendorfer,
she thinks she hears the last few bars
of something—Brahms's *Futile*

Serenade? The boy's tongue feels
warm along her neck, then cold. Warm
then cold in her ear, against her breast.

And as he stalls above her, groaning,
she squeezes his ribs and claws at
his back, transforming his groans

to grunts, his grunts to cries. Tilting
her head, she listens for ghost notes:
a tune left over, a residue of song.

Late Photograph of Whitman

He seems preoccupied with shadows,
      wearing the rueful look
of one who's kept a secret so long
      he has forgotten it.

Nothing like the Sunday-dinner bard
      in that Gilchrist rendering
he hated, "Romeo-curls" of his beard
      puffed up on his chest like a prize collie.

Hunched in his pleated robe, he clutches
      the rocker's arm, gazes
at the camera, placid and self-
      contained, his "chaos of papers"

spilled at his feet. Some unseen
      source of light strikes
his face, illuminates a vase filled
      with lilies just starting to fall apart.

Tall Trees, Still Water

Already the bluish algae
blossom from the river's swill
where the first skunk cabbage waits

to slowly open;
dusk ignites the hill
and touches, for a moment,

everything: deer tracks, this stand
of birch, a pebble in the road—
all the dimmed places—

even the smallest veil-thread
of last season's spider web
trembling in the window of

an abandoned car;
which is all
the wind knows

of what its body looks like:
cow spittle, tension wires,
the legs of a bottle fly.

Man Bathing His Mother

Strange how one can still surprise oneself, even at forty:
    that schoolboy nervousness with which I
        remove my mother's clothes.
            How my eyes

gaze in wonder, even now, at the curls between her thighs.
    The mirror set against another mirror as she
        fidgets in my arms, awaiting
            that first caress.

Watching, listening. What else could I have given her?
    I touch the lines on her belly, the lines
        of my own birth, and repeat the word—
            mother mother:

two shadows moving in accordance, one lurching after
    the other—as I slide a reluctant hand between
        her legs, back into that darkness,
            hapless, brief.

Narcissus

Each day his body, tangled in ferns and larkspur,
      lay elbow deep in summer
when the first wet light of morning touched his face
      and startled him back in love.

Light that must've found him a little stubborn, a little bored,
      in his daze of self-regard.
Light that mistook his stillness as tentative—
      whether it was his own reflection

or if he'd truly thought a beautiful swimming boy
      had moored himself to the bank
where Narcissus dozed, moved only when he moved,
      drank only when he drank.

Terminus

A certain traveler who knew many continents was asked what he
found most remarkable of all. He replied: the ubiquity of sparrows.
—Adam Zagajewski

We find ourselves at the close of the nineteenth century, buying sup-
plies. When the mines flooded last spring, the grocer explains, nothing
left but seepage and soggy tailings. Many in town still find the price of
calabash too dear. In the square, two girls giggle at a blind man stum-
bling over raised curbstones. One among us asks: Given the chance to
proliferate an entirely new race, would we choose to withhold essen-
tial knowledge? How to construct a kinetoscope, for instance; which
mushrooms can be eaten, which cannot. Between us, we discover we
know *apricots* in nine languages, *forgiveness* in three. As clouds mount
over the hills, multiply, disperse, we agree we would not want to have
missed so many decorative turnstiles or the hatching of morphidae,
metallic dazzlers. Inside the vivarium, many have left cocoons. We
lean against the glass and wait for their wings to dry.

Habitation of the Moon

Soon he would have to buckle to and start
eating, drinking, sleeping, and putting
his clothes on in quite alien surroundings.
—Samuel Beckett, *Murphy*

And yet it seemed a concept simple enough:
to leave a place he had no particular love for
and trade it for another, equally loveless.

There were his books to consider, other personal effects:
his shoeboxes filled with postcards he'd sent to himself,
the tatty recliner he'd rescued from the dump

that sang from every hinge each time he sat.
Days, he amused himself with simple thoughts
of the jaunts he'd take to the grand craters,

where he'd stand with his modestly attractive wife
as she fingered the wooden stem of her parasol.
They'd watch moon blossoms shake from moon-tree boughs,

nuzzling their nights away in the shadowy highlands,
roaming each day that minimalist landscape
where little bloomed or faded, that desert of basalts

into which each footfall left a lasting impression,
making it difficult to lose each other
and nearly impossible to disappear.

Notes

1. "The Blind Hunter" was inspired by the article, "Blind Hunter Bags his Second Buck," by Paula Evans Neuman.
2. "Lehinch" from "Snapshots 2" is the name of a village near Claremorris, County Mayo, Ireland. *Poitín* is a home-made Irish liquor distilled from potatoes or malted barley.
3. "Near the Fountain of Tears" owes much to Leslie Stainton's biography, *Lorca: A Dream of Life* (Farrar, Straus, Giroux, 1999).
4. In "Late Fugue, or Poem Ending with a Phrase by Marvin Bell," the phrase "a residue of song" was taken from the title of a 1974 collection of poems by Bell.
5. The epigraph to "Terminus" is from Zagajewski's *Another Beauty* (Farrar, Straus, Giroux, 1998), translated by Clare Cavanagh.

About the Author

Brian Brodeur was born in Worcester, Massachusetts. His poems have appeared in *Crab Orchard Review, Gettysburg Review, Margie, Meridian, New Orleans Review, Pleiades, River Styx, Smartish Pace,* and the anthology *Best New Poets 2005* (Samovar Press, 2005). Brian is the author of *So the Night Cannot Go on without Us* (2007), winner of the Fall 2006 White Eagle Coffee Store Press Chapbook Contest. *Other Latitudes* is his first full-length collection. Brian lives and works in Fairfax, Virginia.

About the Book

Other Latitudes was designed and typeset by Amy Freels. The typeface, Minion, was designed by Robert Slimbach in 1990 for Adobe Systems.

    Other Latitudes was printed on sixty pound Natural Offset and bound by McNaughton & Gunn of Saline, Michigan.